Animal Peculiarity Volume 2 Part 7

By T.P Just

~~~

I0436334

Get All The Books In The Series:

Table of Contents

1. Introduction

The unique characteristics of animals is a miscellany of facts, genuine or supposed, gleamed from earlier and contemporary Greek writers (No Latin writer is once named) and to a limited extent from his own observation to illustrate the habits of the animal world.

We are of course prepared to encounter much that modern science rejects, but the general tone with its search after the picturesque, the startling, even the miraculous, would justify us in ranking Aelian with the paradoxical, rather than with the sober exponents of natural history.

Mythology, mariners' yarns, vulgar superstitions, the ascertained facts of nature—all serve to adorn a tale and, on occasion, to point a moral. His religion is the popular stoicism of the age. Aleian repeatedly affirms his belief in the gods and in divine providence; the wisdom and beneficence of Nature are held up to veneration; the folly and selfishness of man are contrasted with the untaught virtues of the animal world. Some animals, to be sure, have their failings, but he chooses rather to dwell upon their good qualities, devotion, courage, self-sacrifice, gratitude. Again, animals are guided by reason, and from them we may learn contentment, control of the passions, and calm in the face of death

His primary object is to entertain and while so doing to convey instruction in the most agreeable form. Some might find fault with his random and piece-meal handling of his theme-of which he is well aware, and he defends himself with the plea that a frequent change of topic helps to maintain the reader's interest and saves him from boredom.

As to the permanent value of his work he has no misgivings and since we have been informed that his writings were much admired, we may assume that they appealed to cultivated circles in a way that the voluminous and possibly arid compilations of grammarians did not.

Now I am well aware of the labour that others have expended on this subject, yet I have collected all the materials that I could; I have clothed them in untechnical language, and am persuaded that my achievement is a treasure far from negligible. So if anyone considers them profitable, let him make use of them; anyone who does not consider them so may give them to his father to keep and attend to.

2. The Sheep

It seems that Sheep are in fact the most readily obedient of animals and have been taught by Nature to submit to rule. At all events they give heed to the shepherd and his dogs, and they even follow goats.

Also they are devoted to one another and consequently less exposed to the attacks of wolves. For a Sheep does not wander away by itself, nor yet does it separate itself from its fellow, as goats do. The Arabians maintain that their flocks grow fat upon music rather than upon fodder. They like eating saline things, because they add a flavour to their drink. Moreover Sheep know this too, that the north wind and the south wind, no less than the rams which mount them, are their allies in promoting fertility. And this also they know that whereas the north wind tends to produce males, the south wind produces females. And a Sheep that is being covered faces in this direction or in that according as it wants a male or a female offspring.

So Achilles needed to pray in order that his friend lying on the pyre might be burned, and Iris summoned the winds for him, O noble Homer promising them, if they came, a sacrifice by way of reward.

And the son of Neocles taught the Athenians to sacrifice to the winds. But Sheep without any trouble have them ready and unsummoned to help them to pregnancy. And so shepherds also are good at looking out for them, at any rate when the south wind blows they put the rams to the Sheep, in order that their offspring may preferably be female.

3. Icarius and the Hound of Erigone

When Icarius was slain by the relatives of those who, after drinking wine for the first time, fell asleep (for as yet they did not know that what had happened was not death but a drunken stupor), the people of Attica suffered from a disease, Dionysus thereby (as I think) avenging the first and the most elderly man who cultivated his plants.

At any rate the Pythian oracle declared that if they wanted to be restored to health they must offer sacrifice to Icarius and to Erigone his daughter and to her hound which was celebrated for having in its excessive love for its mistress declined to outlive her.

Euripides is not serious when he says "for where is the man who died in consequence of his master's death," although this is what a dog--a slave did ?

A faithful Hound

Now here is a further testimony to the peculiar goodwill which Dogs bear towards those who keep them. A man of Colophon arrived at Teos with the intention of buying up certain articles, for he was a merchant and made his profits by retailing and ex- changing his purchases.

And he brought with him money, a servant, and a Dog; and the slave carried the money. But on the journey the servant stepped aside-he had a pressing call of nature-and the Dog followed him. Now the young man put down the money-bag and forgot to pick it up again and went on his way.

But the Dog lay down on the money and remained quietly there. And when the master and his servant arrived at Teos they returned without doing any business, not having the means to make purchases.

They turned aside however along the same road where the servant left the purse and found their own Dog lying upon it and hardly breathing from starvation. But directly the Dog saw its master and its fellow-slave it moved off the money-bag and in the same instant gave up its post of guardian and its life.

So then even the dog Argus, O divine Homer, was no fiction of yours, no poetical exaggeration, if indeed the events which I have narrated really befell the man of Teos.

4. The Flying Crab

Here is a species of Crab called Peteliae (flyers) .They are paler in appearance than other crabs and are generated in the mud. And when scared they actually fly, for they possess tiny wings which give them a slight lift and lessen their Weight.
When walking however they have no need of them, but when frightened these wings afford them a certain not very considerable assistance, for as they do not fly high and are unable to travel through the air, they are caught; and some people eat these crabs. And they do say that they are good for sciatica if eaten during an attack.

The Hermit crab

Hermit-crabs are born without a shell and select for themselves the shell that makes the best house for them to live in. They even enter the shell of the purple-shell fish if they can find one empty, and the shell of the-whelk.

And so long as it is large enough to cover them they are satisfied with their lodging. But if their body grows they migrate to another dwelling, and they find quantities of such shells.

5. The King Whelk

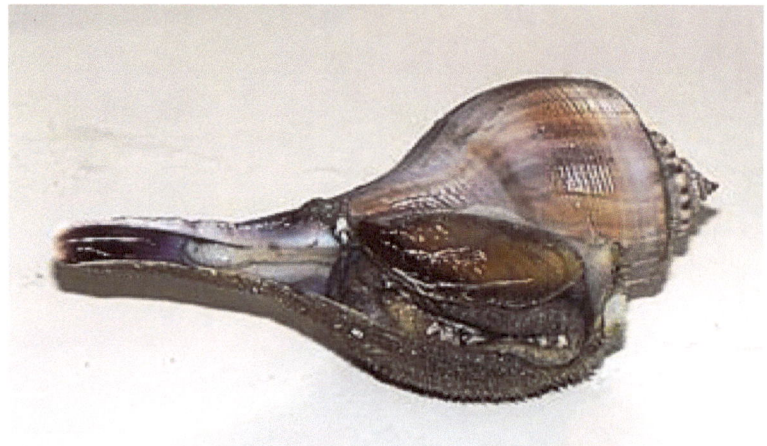

Whelks even have a King and submit most obediently to his rule. And this King exceeds all others in size and beauty. And if it is expedient for him to sink, he is the first to do so; if to come up again, he leads the way; and when, he moves to another place the rest follow him.

The man who succeeds in catching this King knows well- that his affairs will prosper. Moreover if a man sees a King Whelk being caught, he goes away in more cheerful spirits, imagining that he too will have some good fortune.

And at Byzantium a prize is offered for the man who catches the aforesaid fish: each of his fellow-anglers contributes an Attic drachma to the one who catches it, and that is the prize.

6. The Sea-Urchin

Waves roll Sea-urchins out of their haunts, dash them on to the dry land, and hurl them with the utmost violence out of the sea. So for fear of this, whenever these creatures perceive the waves rippling and beginning to swell to greater violence, they pick up with their prickles as many pebbles as they can carry and have some ballast, so that they are not easily rolled about and do not undergo what they dread.

7. The Scolopendra

The Scolopendra is a creature of the sea and looks exactly like the land-Scolopendra (centipede). And if a man's skin come in contact with it, he at once feels a stinging and irritation, and has the same kind of pain as from the plant they call the nettle. And Sea-anemones also produce an itching, but not so violent; and they are better to eat when the equinox is past.

8. A Stampede of Elephants

Whenever Elephants are routed by hunters and begin to stampede like soldiers in war, they do not scatter and take to flight singly but in a herd, and they press against one another as they cling to their fellows.

Round the outside are the young animals, the most pugnacious, you might say; in the middle the old elephants and the mothers, and beneath them they baby elephants, each mother hiding her own. And these little ones are very seldom to be seen.

And even lions, if they catch sight of them herded together, lions which up to that moment have inspired fear and consternation, either flee at full speed or cower down one here and another there, like fawns, in terror of the Elephants. The Elephant does not turn and face its pursuers, unless it be to protect its young or sick ones: then it is irresistible.

Porus and his Elephant

When Porus the King of the Indians had received many wounds in the battle against Alexander, his Elephant proceeded with its trunk to pick out the javelins gently and cautiously; and in spite of its own numerous wounds it did not pause until it knew that its master was collapsing through copious loss of blood and was swooning.

And so it lay down beneath him and remained crouching to prevent Porus from falling from a height and damaging his body even more.

9. Dog as King

I have heard that there is ad race of beings in Ethiopia among whom a Dog is king, and they obey his wishes: when he whimpers they know that he is in p a good temper, but when he barks they understand that he is angry.

If Hermippus is in anyone's view a competent authority, he should carry conviction from having cited Aristocreon as a witness to his story. This has not escaped my notice and it was opportune that I remembered it.

The Dog as Companion

Their hounds used to accompany the people of Hyrcania and Magnesia to war, and in fact these allies were an advantage and a help to them.

An Athenian took with him a Dog as fellow—soldier to the battle of Marathon and both are figured in a painting in the Stoa Poecile, nor was the Dog denied honour but received the reward of the danger it had undergone in being seen among the companions of Cynegirus Epizelus, and Callimachus.

They and the Dog were painted by Micon though some say it was not his work but that of Polygnotus f of Thasos.

The Dog's devotion to its master

Now here are further instances afforded by Dogs of loyalty unsurpassable. When Polus tragic actor died and his body was burning, the Dog which he had kept sprang on to the pyre and was burned to death along with him.

When the body of Mentor was burning, his Eretrian Hounds of their own accord were burned to death and shared his end. Theodorus an excellent harp-player was placed in the coffin by his relatives, and his Maltese Lap-dog threw itself into the receptacle and was buried along with him.

10. Lacydes and his Goose

Lacydes the peripatetic philosopher possessed a remarkable goose. At any rate it was deeply devoted to its keeper: when he went for a walk, it went too; when he sat down, it would remain still and would not leave him for a moment. And when it died Lacydes gave it a most costly funeral as though he were burying a son or a brother.

Pyrrhus and his Elephant

And Pyrrhus of Epirus had an elephant which was so fond of its master that when Pyrrhus was killed at Argos, though its driver had fallen off, it would not halt and remain still until it had rescued him from the hands of the enemy and had brought him back to his friends.

11. Thales and his Mule

Thales of Miletus repaid the malice of a Mule which he detected with great subtlety. A Mule was carrying a load of salt and once, when crossing a river, by accident stumbled and was upset.

Consequently the salt was soaked and melted, and the Mule was delighted to be eased of its burden. So the Mule realising the difference between labour and relaxation took a lesson for the future from its accident and deliberately contrived what before it had unwillingly undergone.

It was impossible for the muleteer to drive it by any other road away from the river. So when Thales heard the man's explanation, he thought that he must contrive to punish the Mule for its malice and ordered the man to load it with sponges and wool on top of the salt.

But the Mule all unaware of the plot stumbled as usual, and having saturated its burden with water, realised that its trick was turned to its own undoing; so after that it made the crossing without disturbance and kept control of its legs and preserved the salt undamaged.

12. Elephant and flower-seller

I learn that at Antioch in Syria there was a tame Elephant and that as it went to its feeding- grounds it used to take great pleasure in the sight of a woman who sold garlands, and would stand close by her and clean her face with its trunk. Accordingly the woman used to hang out as a bait to charm it a garland woven of the season's flowers, and every day it was the Elephant's practice to accept, and hers to offer it. In course of time the woman departed this life, and the Elephant, missing its customary fare and not seeing the woman of its desire, grew savage like a lover who has lost his loved one. And the creature that till then had been of the gentlest was inflamed with passion like men who are over- whelmed with excess of grief and driven out of their senses.

The Elephant, a sun-worshipper

Elephants do obeisance to the rising sun by lifting their trunks like hands to face its beams, and that, you see, is why they are beloved of the god.

Let Ptolemy Philopator be a trustworthy witness to the fact. With the aid of the god he overcame Antiochus," and in sacrificing for his victory and to propitiate the Sun he not only offered sacrifices on a magnificent scale but even went so far as to offer four of the very largest elephants as victims, paying homage, as he supposed, to the god by this very sacrifice.

But a vision in his sleep troubled him: the god seemed to threaten him for this unusual and strange offering. And he in his fear caused four elephants to be made of bronze and offered them to the god in place of those he had slaughtered, hoping to placate him and to ensure his favour.

Elephants for their part worship the gods, whereas mankind is in doubt whether in fact there are gods, and, if there are, whether they take thought for us.

Egyptian priests and their ablutions

The Priests of Egypt do not purify themselves with water of every kind, nor even with such water as they may chance upon, but only with that from which they believe an Ibis has drunk.

For they know full well that this bird would never drink water that was dirty or that had been tainted with any drugs; for they believe that the bird possesses a certain prophetic faculty, seeing that it is sacred.

The Elephant as surgeon

I learn that unwounded Elephants pick spears and javelins out of those that have been wounded, with caution, just as though they understood the practice of surgery and had acquired skill in these matters.

Nicknames

It seems that people in olden times paid regard even to brute beasts in the following way. Pyrrhus of Epirus delighted to be called the Eagle,' and Antiochus, so it is said, to be called 'the Hawk.' I have mentioned these cases together, different though they are; an intelligent man will find them worth knowing.

Mithridates, his body-guard

Mithridates of Pontus when asleep was unwilling to entrust his own safety to weapons and spearmen, and for that reason he kept as body- guard a bull, a horse, and a stag that had been tamed.

Accordingly these animals guarded him while he slept, and if ever anyone approached they at once perceived it by his breathing. And they would wake the King, the bull by bellowing, the horse by neighing, and the stag by bleating.

13. Indian Hounds bred from tigers

Indian histories teach us the following facts also. Huntsmen take thoroughbred bitches which are good at tracking wild animals and are very swift of foot to places infested by these animals; they tie them to trees and then go away, simply, as the saying is, trying a throw of the dice.

And if tigers find them when they have caught nothing and are famished, they tear them to pieces. If however they arrive on heat and full-fed they couple with the bitches, for tigers too when gorged turn their thoughts to sexual inter- course. From this union, so it is said, a tiger is born, not a hound.

And from this tiger and a bitch again a tiger would be born, although the offspring of this last and of a bitch takes after its dam, and the seed degenerates and a hound is born. Nor will Aristotle contradict this.

Now these hounds which can boast a tiger for sire scorn to pursue a stag or to face a boar, but are glad to rush at lions and thereby to give proof of their pedigree. At any rate the Indians gave Alexander the son of Philip a test of the strength of these hounds in the following manner.

They let loose a stag, and the Hound stayed quiet; then a boar and it never moved; after that a bear, but the bear caused it no excitement whatever. But when a lion was let loose, and as though it had seen its real adversary, it neither hesitated nor remained still but leapt upon the lion and clung to it with a vigorous grip, pressing and throttling it.

So then the Indian, who was giving the King this exhibition, knowing full well the Hound's power of endurance, ordered the men to cut off its tail. The tail was cut off, but the Hound paid no heed. So the Indian ordered one of its legs to be cut off, and cut off it was.

But the Hound clung as fast as ever, and would not let go, as though the leg of some other creature unconnected with it were being cut off. Then another leg was cut off and still the Hound would not relax its bite; then a third and it continued to cling; and after these the fourth and still it was capable of biting.

And finally they severed the rest of its body from its head. But the Hound's fangs maintained their original grip, while the head hung aloft on the lion, although the biter himself was no more. At this Alexander was grieved and amazed that the Hound in giving proof of its mettle had perished, a fate the reverse of a coward's, and had met its death by reason of its courage.

Accordingly the Indian seeing Alexander's grief presented him with four hounds of the same breed. And he was delighted to receive them and gave the Indian a suitable gift in return. And when the son of Philip received the four he forgot his grief over the first.

14. The Hound's delight in hunting

Every Hound that is good at hunting delights to catch unaided a wild animal and regards the catch as its prize provided its master consents to this. Otherwise it preserves the animal alive until the huntsman comes up and decides what he wants to do with the capture.
But if it comes upon a dead hare or boar it will not touch it, refusing to claim credit for another's labours and declining to appropriate what does not belong to it. From these facts it appears to have a certain natural love of distinction. It is not meat that it wants; it is victory that it loves.

And it is worth hearing how the Hound behaves when it is hunting." It goes ahead of the huntsman, to whom it is attached by a long leash, and controlling its bark, tracks the game by scent. And so long as no game comes its way and it finds nothing, it goes forward rather despondently to judge from its looks; for all that, it goes ahead and leads the huntsman on with the utmost keenness and pertinacity.

But if it tracks out some beast and comes upon some scent, then it halts. And the huntsman approaches while the Hound overjoyed at its good luck fawns upon its master, licks his feet, and resumes its original quest, advancing step by step until it comes upon the lair; further it does not go.

So then the huntsman understands and with a low, call gives the signal to the men with the nets. And they set the nets in a ring. Thereupon the Hound barks. The intention of its baying just then is to provoke the boar to rise in order that he may emerge and as he flees may be caught in the nets.

And when the beast is captured, the Hound raises a loud cry of victory, as it were a hymn of praise, and is delighted and leaps about, like soldiers who have overcome their enemies. This is what Hounds do in dealing with boars and stags.

15. The Dolphin, its gratitude

It seems that even Dolphins are more scrupulous than men in showing their gratitude and are not con- trolled by the Persian custom applauded by Xenophon And what I have to tell is as follows.

One Coeranus by name, a native of Paros, when some Dolphins fell into the net and were captured at Byzantium, gave their captors money, as it were a ransom, and set them at liberty; and for this he earned their gratitude.

At any rate he was sailing once (so the story goes) in a fifty-oar ship with a crew of Milesians, when the ship cap- sized in the strait between Naxos and Paros, and though all the rest were drowned, Coeranus was rescued by Dolphins which repaid the good deed that he had first done them by a similar deed.

And the headland and caverned rock to which they swam with him on their backs are pointed out, and the spot is called Coeraneus. Later when this same Coeranus died they burnt his body by the sea-shore.

Where- upon the Dolphins, observing this from some point, assembled as though they were attending his funeral and all the while that the pyre was ablaze they remained at hand, as one trusty friend might remain by another.

When at length the fire was quenched they swam away. Men however are subservient to the wealthy and the seemingly prosperous while they are alive, but when dead or in misfortune they turn their backs upon them so as to avoid repaying them for past favours

16. Tame Fishes

It seems that even Fishes are both tame and tractable, and when summoned can hear and are ready to accept food that is given them, like the sacred eel in the Fountain of Arethusa. And men tell of the moray belonging to Crassus b the Roman, which had been adorned with earrings and small necklaces set with jewels, just like some lovely maiden; and when Crassus called it, it would recognise his voice and come swimming up, and whatever he offered it, it would eagerly and promptly take and eat.

Now when this fish died Crassus, so I am told, actually mourned for it and buried it. And on one occasion when Domitius said to him 'You fool, mourning for a dead moray! ' Crassus took him up with these words: 'I mourned for a moray, but you never mourned for the three wives you buried.'

Get All The Books In The Series:

www.ingramcontent.com/pod-product-compliance
Lightning Source LLC
Chambersburg PA
CBHW050919290526
45792CB00002B/815